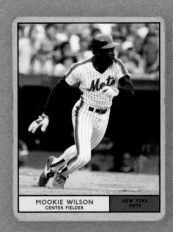

MOOKIE WILSON
CENTER FIELDER

NEW YORK
METS

TOM SEAVER
PITCHER

NEW YORK
METS

THE STORY OF THE NEW YORK METS

Published by Creative Paperbacks
P.O. Box 227, Mankato, Minnesota 56002
Creative Paperbacks is an imprint of The Creative Company
www.thecreativecompany.us

Design and production by Blue Design
Art direction by Rita Marshall
Printed by Corporate Graphics in the United States of America

Photographs by Getty Images (Al Bello, Bruce Bennett Studio, Andrew D. Bernstein, Linda Cataffo/NY Daily News Archive, Ed Clarity/NY Daily News Archive, C. Taylor Crothers, Stephen Dunn, Don Emmert/ AFP, G Flume, Focus on Sport, Doug Kanter/AFP, Lass, David Leeds/Allsport, Jim McIsaac, National Baseball Hall of Fame Library/MLB Photos, Rich Pilling/MLB Photos, Louis Requena/MLB Photos, Ezra Shaw, Keith Torrie/NY Daily News Archive, Chris Trotman, Ron Vesely/MLB Photos, Michael Zagaris/ MLB Photos)

The Library of Congress has cataloged the hardcover edition as follows:

Goodman, Michael E.
The story of the New York Mets / by Michael E. Goodman.
p. cm. — (Baseball: the great American game)
Includes index.
Summary: The history of the New York Mets professional baseball team from its inaugural 1962 season to today, spotlighting the team's greatest players and most memorable moments.
ISBN 978-1-60818-048-6 (hardcover)
ISBN 978-0-89812-646-4 (pbk)
1. New York Mets (Baseball team)—History—Juvenile literature. I. Title. II. Title: New York Mets. III. Series.

GV875.N45G68 2011
796.357'64097471—dc22   2010025207

CPSIA: 031212 PO1556

9 8 7 6 5 4 3 2

Page 3: Right fielder Darryl Strawberry
Page 4: Shortstop Jose Reyes

BASEBALL: THE GREAT AMERICAN GAME

THE STORY OF THE NEW YORK METS

Michael E. Goodman

CREATIVE
PAPER BACKS

CONTENTS

LOVABLE LOSERS

In 1609, British adventurer Henry Hudson, sailing on behalf of a Dutch trading company, crossed the Atlantic Ocean and explored the American coast from what is now Maine to New York. This area was, in his words, "as pleasant a land as one can tread upon." Hudson's positive reports convinced a group of Dutch settlers in 1624 to establish the colony of New Amsterdam along the mid-Atlantic coast. The British took over New Amsterdam in the 1660s and renamed it to honor the Duke of York. Although New York City was located in the northern part of the United States, it quickly grew to become the country's center of business, culture, and media.

New York also became an important American center for sports, especially baseball. In 1883, a professional team called the New York Metropolitans was established as part of an early league, the American Association. That franchise lasted for only a few years, but its name was revived in 1962, when Major League Baseball agreed to establish a new National League (NL) team in New York. The Metropolitans, or

A major hub for American business and culture, New York City is also a sports mecca, hosting at least one franchise in all of the major professional sports.

PITCHER · TOM SEAVER

A golden boy from Southern California, Tom Seaver brought to New York an amazing blend of power and accuracy. His pitches exploded at the plate, putting hitters at his mercy. During his 20-year career, he won 311 games, established a big-league record by striking out 200 or more batters 9 years in a row, and captured 3 Cy Young Awards as the league's best pitcher. When he was elected to the Hall of Fame in 1992, Seaver received the highest percentage of votes (98.84%) of any player in baseball history. Since 1999, he has served as a television announcer and front-office executive with the Mets.

TOM SEAVER
PITCHER

NEW YORK
METS

STATS

Mets seasons: 1967–77, 1983

Height: 6-foot-1

Weight: 210

- **61 career complete-game shutouts**

- **3,640 career strikeouts**

- **12-time All-Star**

- **Baseball Hall of Fame inductee (1992)**

"Mets" for short, filled a painful void that had been created for local sports fans when two longtime NL franchises—the Brooklyn Dodgers and New York Giants—moved to California in 1958. New York fans were thrilled to once again have a local NL club opposite the Yankees of the American League (AL).

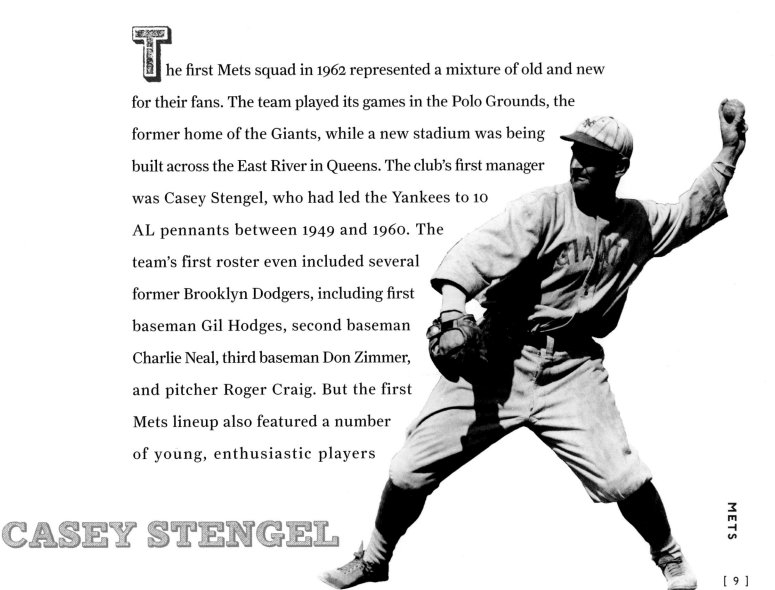

The first Mets squad in 1962 represented a mixture of old and new for their fans. The team played its games in the Polo Grounds, the former home of the Giants, while a new stadium was being built across the East River in Queens. The club's first manager was Casey Stengel, who had led the Yankees to 10 AL pennants between 1949 and 1960. The team's first roster even included several former Brooklyn Dodgers, including first baseman Gil Hodges, second baseman Charlie Neal, third baseman Don Zimmer, and pitcher Roger Craig. But the first Mets lineup also featured a number of young, enthusiastic players

CASEY STENGEL

who quickly captured the hearts of fans in New York. These included 17-year-old first baseman Ed Kranepool, catcher Clarence "Choo Choo" Coleman, and shortstop Elio Chacon.

One thing that both veteran and inexperienced Mets players had in common in the team's early years was incompetence. The Mets had trouble doing anything right, and the club piled up loss after loss. Still, their fans adored them. The Mets faithful had special affection for first baseman Marv Throneberry, whom they lovingly called "Marvelous Marv." Throneberry played only two seasons with the Mets, but his muffs in the field and on the base paths became legendary. One game, he hit a triple to drive in two runs but was called out for failing to touch first base on his way to third. When Stengel came out of the dugout to argue, the umpire told him, "Don't bother, Casey. He missed second base, too." By season's end, the Mets had established a major-league record for losses in a season (120) while winning just 40 games. But Stengel remained optimistic, even dubbing his players "The Amazin's" for winning as many games as they did.

The Mets continued to lose for the next five seasons as well, though they were seldom blown out of games. Instead, they would tantalize

POLO GROUNDS

New York's famous Polo Grounds went through several dramatic transformations in the late 1800s and early 1900s, going from a simple field designed for the horseback sport of polo to the aging but revered stadium the Mets moved into in 1962.

WORST EVER?

The 1962 Mets set a major-league record for futility, losing 120 games, but were they the worst team ever? They certainly did a lot of things poorly. Asked early on in the season where he thought his club would finish, manager Casey Stengel replied, "We'll finish in Chicago." The year got off to a bad start with a rainout on opening day in St. Louis. That was followed by nine straight losses. The losses kept piling up, and the team was mathematically eliminated from any chance to win the pennant on August 7—the earliest that had ever

happened in baseball history. The club had 2 pitchers with 20 or more losses and only 1 pitcher who won at least 10 games. That was veteran Roger Craig, a former Brooklyn Dodgers hurler, who finished with a dismal 10–24 record. Still, nearly a million baseball-starved NL fans in and around "The Big Apple" turned out to see the Mets play at the Polo Grounds that year. Stengel knew who the real stars were in 1962. "The fans were marvelous," he said. "They came out and did better than we did on the field, and I'm glad we've got them."

CATCHER · MIKE PIAZZA

Mike Piazza was not the best catcher in baseball history. His arm was merely average, and in four different seasons, he led all NL catchers in errors behind the plate. But defense wasn't Piazza's game. His ticket to stardom was a booming bat, which he used to bash more home runs than any other big-league backstop. He joined the Mets at the peak of his offensive powers, driving in a career-high 124 runs during the 1999 season. Throughout his 16-year career in the majors, Piazza collected 10 Silver Slugger awards as the league's top-hitting catcher.

MIKE PIAZZA
CATCHER

NEW YORK
METS

STATS

Mets seasons: 1998–2005

Height: 6-foot-3

Weight: 200

- 427 career HR

- .308 career BA

- 1993 NL Rookie of the Year

- 12-time All-Star

FIRST BASEMAN · KEITH HERNANDEZ

No first baseman has ever covered ground in the field like Keith Hernandez. Taking a position far off the bag, Hernandez made sure nothing could get past him on either side. He was also famous for making kamikaze rushes toward the plate to smother sacrifice bunting attempts. Hernandez was no slouch on offense, either. He topped the .300 mark six times in his career and ranks third on the Mets' all-time list in batting average. Nicknamed "Mex" because of his Mexican heritage, Hernandez remained a familiar face in New York as a Mets broadcaster and as an advertising spokesman.

KEITH HERNANDEZ
FIRST BASEMAN

NEW YORK
METS

STATS

Mets seasons: 1983–89

Height: 6 feet

Weight: 195

- 11-time Gold Glove winner

- 2,182 career hits

- .296 career BA

- 1,071 career RBI

their fans by keeping contests close, only to find an unusual way to succumb in the end. As lovable losers, the Mets provided a sharp contrast to the Yankees, who were perennial, almost monotonous winners, and this difference seemed to add to their appeal among young New Yorkers. Starting in 1964, those fans packed newly built Shea Stadium, screaming "Let's go, Mets!" at the top of their lungs and praying for victories.

BELIEVING IN MIRACLES

 ventually, the Mets and their fans grew tired of losing. The original Mets were slowly replaced by hungry young players who were eager to establish a winning reputation. Even Casey Stengel stepped down as manager in 1965. By the mid-1960s, the New York lineup featured such solid performers as shortstop Bud Harrelson, outfielder Cleon Jones, and catcher Jerry Grote. Then the Mets won a special lottery to acquire superstar college pitcher George Thomas Seaver.

Seaver had a great fastball, a solid curve, and an intense desire to win.

He was different from any pitcher Mets fans had seen so far on their team, and he soon earned the nickname "Tom Terrific." During his rookie season in 1967, Seaver recorded 16 wins and 170 strikeouts. The next year, he was joined by lefty curveball expert Jerry Koosman and right-handed fireballer Nolan Ryan, giving New York one of the top pitching staffs in the NL.

The Mets now had a nucleus of fine players but needed a dynamic new manager to drive them to victory. That leader was Gil Hodges, one of the original Mets and, before that, a 16-year veteran with the Dodgers in Brooklyn and Los Angeles. New York baseball fans knew and loved Hodges, and he paid back their devotion by promising that the Mets would win at least 70 games in 1968 and break the .500 mark soon after.

Seaver and Koosman did their part, combining for 35 wins during the 1968 season, and the club achieved a best-ever 73–89 finish. Then, early the next season, a Seaver victory brought the Mets to the magic .500 level for the first time. After battling with the Chicago Cubs for much of the year, the Mets won 38 of their last 49 games to blow past the Cubs and capture the NL Eastern Division championship. With

JERRY KOOSMAN

SECOND BASEMAN · EDGARDO ALFONZO

"Fonzie" broke in with the Mets as a third baseman and was later switched to second. A spray hitter with surprising power, Alfonzo ranks in the Mets' all-time Top 10 in home runs, RBI, total bases, extra-base hits, batting average, games played, at bats, runs, hits, and doubles. In 1999, Alfonzo teamed with shortstop Rey Ordoñez, third baseman Robin Ventura, and first baseman John Olerud to form what *Sports Illustrated* called "The Best Infield Ever." Alfonzo's clutch hitting in the postseason led the Mets to key victories in their pennant drives in 1999 and 2000 and forever endeared him to Mets fans.

EDGARDO ALFONZO
SECOND BASEMAN

NEW YORK
METS

STATS

Mets seasons: 1995–2002

Height: 5-foot-11

Weight: 185

- **146 career HR**

- **744 career RBI**

- **.284 career BA**

- **.444 BA in 2000 NLCS**

a 25–7 record, 208 strikeouts, and a 2.21 earned run average (ERA), Seaver easily won the 1969 NL Cy Young Award as the league's best pitcher, while Koosman and Ryan combined for 23 more wins. Asked by a reporter about the team's amazing turnaround, Hodges said, "I really didn't think we'd come as far as we have as fast as we have, but now that we're here, I see no reason to stop."

Neither did his players. In the NL Championship Series (NLCS), the underdog Mets continued to roll, sweeping the Atlanta Braves in three straight games. Then it was on to the World Series to face the Baltimore Orioles, a team that is still widely regarded as one of the best in baseball history. But no team was a match for the "Miracle Mets" of 1969. Time after time, New York players made clutch hits and remarkable fielding plays to propel the Mets over the Orioles in five games. Unbelievably, the once-laughable Mets were world champs!

Over the next few years, the Mets' pitching remained strong, but their hitting fizzled, and the club had trouble winning consistently. Then another miracle occurred. The Mets were in last place in the NL East on August 1, 1973, when several fans asked fiery relief pitcher Tug McGraw, "What's wrong with the Mets?" McGraw responded, "There's nothing wrong with the Mets. You gotta believe!"

DAVID VERSUS GOLIATH

The Mets' magical ride to the 1969 world championship may have been the most improbable in baseball history. In their first 7 seasons, the Mets had never finished higher than 9th in the 10-team NL. In 1969, the NL was split into two divisions, with two teams qualifying for the playoffs. The Mets put together a strong finish to capture the NL East that year and earn a berth in the first-ever NLCS against the Atlanta Braves. Although the Braves featured such feared hitters as Hank Aaron and Orlando Cepeda, the Mets' bats dominated during a three-game New York sweep. Then it was off to Baltimore to face an Orioles club that had topped the AL in batting, fielding, and pitching. The heavily favored Orioles started quickly when outfielder Don Buford led off Game 1 with a home run to trigger a 4–1 Baltimore victory. Amazingly, the Orioles would not win again. The Mets made all of the big plays in the field and at bat to capture the series four games to one. In a strange twist, the final Orioles player to make an out was second baseman Davey Johnson, who would later manage the Mets to a World Series triumph in 1986.

McGraw repeated the battle cry to his teammates before the game that night and before each contest for the rest of the season. He convinced the Mets to believe, and they stormed back to clinch the division title on the last day of the season. Then they just kept on winning. The Mets outdueled Cincinnati's star-studded "Big Red Machine" lineup for the NL pennant and battled the defending champion Oakland A's in a closely contested World Series before finally falling in seven games. By the end of 1973, the Mets had made every fan a believer.

EXCELLING IN THE '80s

 nfortunately, the Mets faithful had little to believe in for the next 10 years. The team slid into a decade-long slump, finishing in the NL East cellar five times. Players such as strongman outfielder/first baseman Dave Kingman, popular outfielder Lee Mazzilli, speedy catcher John Stearns, and pitcher Craig Swan performed admirably in Mets blue and orange, but nothing helped the team escape from the bottom of the standings.

THIRD BASEMAN · DAVID WRIGHT

With his rifle arm and powerful bat, David Wright finally ended the Mets' long search for a star third baseman. The young slugger began putting up great numbers as soon as he arrived, topping the .300 mark 5 times, knocking in more than 100 RBI in 4 straight seasons (2005 to 2008), earning 2 Gold Gloves for his fielding, and being named to 5 NL All-Star teams. He impressed Mets coaches and fans both with his talent and his poise. "I'm very confident in what I do," Wright said, "but I'd like to think that I don't show any cockiness or overconfidence."

STATS

Mets seasons: 2004–present

Height: 6 feet

Weight: 200

- **169 career HR**

- **664 career RBI**

- **5-time All-Star**

- **.305 career BA**

DAVID WRIGHT
THIRD BASEMAN

NEW YORK
METS

TOM SEAVER

THE ELUSIVE NO-HITTER

What do Tom Seaver, Nolan Ryan, Warren Spahn, Dwight Gooden, David Cone, and Pedro Martinez have in common—besides all having pitched for the Mets at one time? Each tossed a no-hit, no-run game in his career (and Cone even hurled a perfect game). But none of them achieved this feat while pitching for the Mets. In fact, as of 2010, no Mets pitcher had ever hurled a "no-no" in the team's history. Seaver came the closest, twice taking a no-hitter into the ninth inning, in 1969 and 1972, before the spell was broken. He finally did record a no-hitter in June 1978 as a member of the Cincinnati Reds. Ryan tossed a major-league-record seven no-hit gems during his years with the California Angels, Texas Rangers, and Houston Astros, far from New York. And Cone hurled his perfect game with the Yankees in 1999. Lots of Mets pitchers—22 of them—have recorded complete-game one-hitters: Seaver had five; Cone, Jon Matlack, and Steve Trachsel had two each; and Bobby Jones even threw a one-hit masterpiece against the San Francisco Giants in the 2000 NLDS to help bring New York one step closer to that year's World Series.

A turnaround finally began in 1983. When the club got off to a slow start that year, general manager Frank Cashen brought up minor-leaguer Darryl Strawberry, an outfielder with one of the sweetest, most powerful swings in baseball history. Then, between 1983 and 1985, Cashen engineered a series of trades to surround his young star with proven veterans. In came first baseman Keith Hernandez, a remarkable fielder and dependable hitter; catcher and team leader Gary Carter; and switch-hitting third baseman Howard Johnson.

Cashen then reached again into the club's rich farm system for two outstanding young hurlers, fireballer Dwight "Doc" Gooden and curveball specialist Ron Darling; fiery second baseman Wally Backman; and even the club's new manager, former major-league second baseman Davey Johnson. Suddenly, all the pieces were in place for another championship run. Mets fans got a preview in 1985, when the 20-year-old Gooden posted a sensational 24–4 record with a 1.53 ERA. With Carter, Hernandez, and Strawberry leading a revitalized offense, the Mets finished a close second to the St. Louis Cardinals in the NL East.

In 1986, the Mets won a team-record 108 games and ran away with the

NL East title. Then they edged past the Houston Astros in six games in the NLCS—rallying twice in the ninth inning of contests and twice in extra innings—in one of the most exciting playoff series of all time.

Still, those miracle endings were nothing compared with what transpired in the sixth game of the World Series against the Boston Red Sox. In the 10th inning, Boston was one out away from capturing the series before a wild pitch allowed the Mets to score the tying run. A bad-hop grounder hit by outfielder Mookie Wilson then rolled under the glove of Boston first baseman Bill Buckner to bring in the winning run. Two days later, the Mets rallied again in Game 7 to capture their second world championship. "Don't ask me how we did it—mirrors, magic wands, whatever," said Wilson. "What does it matter? We did it!"

After a brief dip in 1987, the Mets made another title run in 1988. The season got off to a great start when Strawberry blasted 2 home runs—1 of which traveled nearly 600 feet—on opening day in Montreal to power New York to a 10–6 win. Gooden won that game, the first of his 18 victories on the year. Newcomer David Cone, a crafty right-hander,

DWIGHT GOODEN

Dwight Gooden blew away batters in his first two big-league seasons; at just 19 and 20 years old, he led the NL in strikeouts in both 1984 and 1985.

SHORTSTOP · BUD HARRELSON

During his career with the Mets, Derrel "Bud" Harrelson was the team's heart. As steady as he was on defense (committing only 209 errors in 16 major-league seasons), the shortstop was even more valuable as a feisty team leader. Harrelson won the lasting love and admiration of Mets fans during the 1973 NLCS against Cincinnati when he exchanged fisticuffs with Pete Rose after the Reds star made a vicious slide into second base. Galvanized by that altercation, the Mets went on to defeat the Reds and reach the World Series. Harrelson later coached for the Mets and managed the club in 1990 and 1991.

BUD HARRELSON
SHORTSTOP

NEW YORK
METS

STATS

Mets seasons: 1965–77

Height: 5-foot-11

Weight: 160

- 45 career triples

- 94 career sacrifice bunts

- 2-time All-Star

- 1971 Gold Glove winner

had an even better season on the mound than Gooden, going 20–3 with a 2.22 ERA. Behind these efforts, the club won 100 games.

In the NLCS, the Mets faced off against the Dodgers, a team they had beaten 10 of 11 times during the regular season. The Mets were confident—perhaps overconfident. After New York took Game 1, Cone boasted to reporters that the Mets were good, but the Dodgers were lucky. His words inspired the Dodgers to prove him wrong, and they roared back to capture the series, four games to three. The Mets had come close, but it would take more than a decade for them to reach the "Fall Classic" again.

ORDERING IN PIAZZA

s the 1980s drew to a close, so did the Mets' reign of dominance over the NL East. By 1993, the club had reached rock bottom again, losing 103 games. "We're just as bad as the old Mets," grumbled manager Dallas Green, "but this time nobody's laughing." So Green and his successor, Bobby Valentine, engineered a rebuilding process.

Mets management put together an outstanding double-play

LEFT FIELDER · RUSTY STAUB

Nicknamed "Le Grande Orange" for his flaming red hair by Expos fans during his early-career years playing in Montreal, Rusty Staub brought skill and flair to New York during two different stints with the Mets. In the 1973 playoffs, he overcame a painful shoulder injury to make several key defensive plays and slam a homer in the World Series against Oakland. In his later years in New York, he specialized in clutch pinch hitting. A master chef as well as a baseball star, Staub ran a successful restaurant in New York during and following his playing days.

RUSTY STAUB
LEFT FIELDER

NEW YORK
METS

STATS

Mets seasons: 1972–75, 1981–85

Height: 6-foot-2

Weight: 220

- 292 career HR

- 2,716 career hits

- 6-time All-Star

- NL-record 25 pinch-hit RBI in 1983

JESSE OROSCO

THE GAME THAT WOULDN'T END

The Independence Day fireworks came late at Atlanta–Fulton County Stadium on July 4, 1985, and weary Mets players and fans were the ones who celebrated. Rain clouds hung over the stadium that night, threatening to cancel both the game between the Mets and Atlanta Braves and the post-game fireworks. The game featured several rain delays and lots of scoring by both teams. By the bottom of the eighth inning, the Mets led 7–4 and brought in their closer, Jesse Orosco, to finish the game. But the lefty reliever gave up four runs, and the Mets had to rally in the ninth to send the game into extra innings long after midnight. When both teams scored twice in the 13th inning, the battle kept going. Five innings and nearly two hours later, New York scratched across a run in the 18th, but that was negated when Mets reliever Tom Gorman gave up an improbable home run to Atlanta pitcher Rick Camp, one of the league's weakest hitters. Finally, in the 19th, the Mets scored 5 times and withstood a furious Braves rally for a 16–13 victory. The game ended at 3:14 A.M., and fireworks lit up the Atlanta sky literally "by the dawn's early light."

METS

combination consisting of
second baseman Edgardo
Alfonzo—an offensive as well as defensive threat—and Gold Glove-
winning shortstop Rey Ordoñez. Another valuable addition was
backstop Todd Hundley, who supplied a power surge by slamming 41
round-trippers in 1996, setting a new major-league record for catchers.

The offense and defense had improved, but pitching remained a problem
for New York until 1997. That year, timely hitting and strong pitching from
starters Rick Reed and Bobby Jones and reliever John Franco helped the
Mets post their first winning record since 1990 (88–74). As the club came
from behind to win a remarkable 47 times, fans started to believe again.

The Mets still lacked a true superstar, however. That changed on
May 22, 1998, when they acquired catcher Mike Piazza from the Florida
Marlins. Piazza, perhaps the best-hitting catcher of all time, arrived
in New York with career averages of 33 homers and 105 runs batted in
(RBI) per year, and he would improve on those marks with the Mets.
Piazza's presence instantly made the club's lineup a dangerous one.
"Mike turns mistakes into misery," said Braves pitcher John Smoltz.
Piazza's majestic drives over the fences at Shea Stadium reminded fans
of Darryl Strawberry's shots a decade earlier.

Piazza, Alfonzo, and first baseman John Olerud spearheaded a New York offense that led the team to second place in the NL East in 1998. The Mets were even better in 1999, winning 97 games and earning the NL Wild Card berth with a one-game playoff win over Cincinnati in which lefty ace Al Leiter hurled a magnificent two-hit shutout. After an NL Division Series (NLDS) rout of the Arizona Diamondbacks, the Mets lost an exciting NLCS battle to Atlanta, four games to two.

New York would not be denied in its pursuit of a pennant in 2000. The Mets finished close behind the Braves during the regular season and captured their second straight Wild Card. This time, they beat the San Francisco Giants and St. Louis Cardinals to reach the World Series, where they faced their crosstown rivals, the two-time defending champion Yankees.

CENTER FIELDER · MOOKIE WILSON

Wilson's given name was William Hayward Wilson, but Mets fans loudly cheered him as "Moooo-kie" during his years in New York. Wilson struck out too often and walked too seldom to be a great leadoff hitter, but he had speed and savvy. That speed also helped him patrol center field at Shea Stadium effectively. Although he was physically gifted, it was Mookie's enthusiasm and sheer love of playing that made him a fan favorite. After his playing days, he served as a first base coach with the Mets for several seasons and then as manager of its minor-league franchise in Brooklyn.

STATS

Mets seasons: 1980–89

Height: 5-foot-10

Weight: 170

- **438 career RBI**

- **71 career triples**

- **4 seasons of 20-plus doubles**

- **327 career stolen bases**

MOOKIE WILSON
CENTER FIELDER

NEW YORK
METS

The clash was the first New York "Subway Series" (so-called because fans could take a subway between the two teams' stadiums) since 1956, when the Brooklyn Dodgers met and lost to the Yankees. The Mets put up a fight through five tense games, but the Yankees captured the series, four games to one. The drama continued to the bitter end, when Yankees center fielder Bernie Williams tracked down a hard shot off Piazza's bat in the ninth inning of Game 5 to stop the Mets from staging a comeback.

The loss seemed to signal the start of another decline for the Mets. The team quickly dropped below .500 again, and management decided to shake things up. First, crafty left-hander Tom Glavine, a former Cy Young Award winner with the Braves, was signed as a free agent in 2003 to anchor the club's pitching staff. Then the Mets promoted shortstop Jose Reyes and third baseman David Wright from the minor leagues to take over the left side of the infield. Reyes's speed and surprising power and Wright's all-around excellence in the field and at bat enhanced Mets fans' confidence that their club would soon be back on top.

PEDRO MARTINEZ

GOOD STARTS, BAD ENDINGS

fter the Mets put together a forgettable 2004 season, Omar Minaya was brought in as general manager to oversee the ongoing rebuilding process. Minaya hired longtime Yankees player and coach Willie Randolph as manager. Then he began wheeling and dealing for new players,

WHO'S ON THIRD?

In 1989, Howard Johnson became the first Mets third baseman to be named to the NL All-Star team. That's probably because so few Mets ever played a full year at the position before Johnson. The team's first starting third-sacker, former Dodgers player Don Zimmer, was traded away early in the 1962 season. His replacement, Charlie Neal, was gone a year later. In their history, the Mets have put more than 130 different players on the "hot corner"—an average of nearly 3 per year. The worst trade in Mets history was made in December 1971 in an attempt to find a solid third baseman, when future Hall of Fame pitcher Nolan Ryan was sent to the Angels in exchange for Jim Fregosi, whose frequent injuries prevented him from playing his best for the Mets. When David Wright took over the position as a rookie in 2004 and became a perennial All-Star in 2006, Mets fans believed the club's search for a top-caliber third baseman had ended at last. While the hot corner has always been a trouble spot in the lineup, the Mets have fared unusually well at catcher. All-Star Mets catchers include Jerry Grote, John Stearns, Gary Carter, Todd Hundley, and Mike Piazza.

RIGHT FIELDER · DARRYL STRAWBERRY

No Mets player had a higher rise or a deeper fall than Darryl Strawberry. His picture-perfect swing and powerful wrists enabled Strawberry to hit majestic home run shots. He made it look easy, perhaps too easy, according to manager Davey Johnson. "He had the swing, the grace, the power," Johnson said. "When he wanted to be, he was as good as it gets."

DARRYL STRAWBERRY
RIGHT FIELDER

NEW YORK
METS

Unfortunately, Strawberry was also plagued by demons. The pressure to succeed in New York drove the shy superstar to alcohol and drugs. Later, he suffered from colon cancer and mood swings that sapped his talent and desire.

STATS

Mets seasons: 1983–90

Height: 6-foot-6

Weight: 200

- 335 career HR

- 1,000 career RBI

- 8-time All-Star

- 1983 NL Rookie of the Year

MANAGER · DAVEY JOHNSON

When he played second base in Baltimore and Atlanta, Davey Johnson was known as a fiery competitor who would push himself beyond his natural talents. (One year, he even out-homered teammate Hank Aaron.) His motto was "Play hard, and play to win." When he took over as Mets manager in 1984, the club needed an injection of that same passion. He replaced some of the staid, aging Mets with eager youngsters, and he got results. The 1984 team was the first Mets club to top the 90-win mark in 15 years. Two years later, the team won 108 games and a world championship.

STATS

Mets seasons as manager: 1984–90

Managerial record: 1,148–888

World Series championship: 1986

DAVEY JOHNSON
MANAGER

NEW YORK
METS

starting by convincing Red Sox pitcher Pedro Martinez to sign with the Mets as a free agent. Martinez brought a devastating curveball, a volatile personality, and extreme confidence to Shea Stadium. He also brought the mindset of a winner. "If I'm going to war in this league," said Minaya, "I want Pedro on my side." Martinez made the signing look good by winning 15 games and striking out more than 200 batters in 2005.

Minaya also added muscle to the Mets' offense by signing multitalented center fielder Carlos Beltran and slugging first baseman Carlos Delgado and shored up the relief pitching corps by obtaining dominant closer Billy Wagner. All of these additions helped make 2006 a special season at Shea Stadium. The Mets charged to an NL-best 97–65 record and then swept the Dodgers in the first round of the playoffs. Their success was a true team effort, as Beltran slugged 41 homers, Delgado clubbed 38, Wright drove in 116 runs, Reyes swiped 64 bases, and Wagner nailed down 40 saves. But the Mets could not quite get to the top, losing to the red-hot Cardinals in a fiercely contested NLCS that went a full seven games.

Minaya predicted even better results in 2007, and early on, his forecast appeared accurate. For five months, Randolph seemed to push all of the right buttons, and the Mets took command of their division, holding a 7-game lead over the second-place Philadelphia Phillies with only 17 games to go in the season. Then, shockingly, the Mets lost 12 of those 17 games in one of the worst collapses in baseball history. Needing a win in the final game of the year to force a one-game playoff with the Phillies, the Mets lost. "It's obviously painful," said Wright. "It hurts. We gradually let this thing slip away."

When the Mets got off to another terrific start in 2008, their fans were ready to forgive them for the 2007 collapse. New star pitcher Johan Santana dominated opposing batters, and Delgado, Beltran, and Wright drove in runs at a furious pace. When the team went through a rocky period in midseason, Randolph was replaced as manager by Jerry Manuel, who pushed the Mets back to the top of the NL East. Then, unbelievably, they stopped winning again. In a replay of 2007, the Mets once again faced a "do-or-die" situation in the last game of the season. And, once again, they failed, falling

2000 WORLD SERIES

NEW YORK, NEW YORK

The Mets and Yankees are big rivals in New York. The clubs faced each other in the 2000 Subway Series and even met in an unusual doubleheader earlier that season, with the first game occurring in the afternoon at Shea Stadium in Queens and the nightcap at Yankee Stadium in the Bronx. That was the first time in nearly 100 years that 2 teams had played 2 games in 1 day in different ballparks. Despite their rivalry, the Mets and Yankees have some interesting connections. More than 90 different players have worn both uniforms during their careers. In addition, six different Mets managers have also served as a manager or coach for the Yankees—from Casey Stengel in 1962 to Willie Randolph in 2005. Other "New York, New York" skippers include Yogi Berra, who led both teams to a World Series; Joe Torre, who won 4 titles with the Yankees and recorded nearly 300 wins with the Mets from 1977 to 1981; and less successful field generals Jeff Torborg and Dallas Green. Players who had outstanding seasons for both the Mets and Yankees included pitchers David Cone and Dwight Gooden; outfielders Rickey Henderson, Lee Mazzilli, and Darryl Strawberry; and third-sacker Robin Ventura.

METS

Famous for his almost unhittable changeup pitch, Johan Santana suited up for New York after winning two Cy Young Awards with the Minnesota Twins.

JOHAN SANTANA

JASON BAY

Despite the efforts of Jason Bay (opposite) and Mike Pelfrey (right), the Mets' 2011 season was a disappointing one, ending with a 77–85 mark.

to the Florida Marlins, 4–2. "We needed one or two hitters to come through," Manuel lamented, "but they didn't."

In 2009, the Mets moved into a new home, Citi Field, with a new sense of confidence. Unfortunately, injuries and disappointing performance led to frustrating losing campaigns both that year and the next two. Still, hope remained high in New York that the Mets would soon bounce back among the NL contenders. Adding to the local optimism was the 2010 acquisition of veteran outfielder Jason Bay, the star potential of young first baseman Ike Davis, and the emergence of talented pitchers Mike Pelfrey and Fernando Nieve.

For 50 years, the Mets have earned the love and devotion of New York baseball fans. They have come a long way since starting out as lovable losers in the early 1960s, capturing World Series trophies in 1969 and 1986 and becoming NL pennant contenders in the 2000s. Today's Mets aim to add to this winning tradition, giving their fans reason to believe that more great times are just around the corner.

INDEX